RONAN FOREVER

pop culture

throb

Copyright © 1998 Pop Culture

All rights reserved. No part of this publication may be reproduced, stored in a retrieval system, or transmitted in any form or by any means, electronic, mechanical, photocopying, recording or otherwise without prior permission of the copyright owners except in the case of brief quotations embodied in critical articles or reviews. A catalogue record for this book is available from the British Library.
Printed in the United Kingdom.

The author and publisher have made every effort to contact all copyright holders. Any, who for whatever reason have not been contacted are invited to write to the publishers so that a full acknowledgement may be made in subsequent editions of this work.

ISBN 1 901827 06 2

Picture credits: All Action, Famous, London Features International Limited, Retna Pictures Limited, Rex Features Ltd., Steve Gillett.
Cover Picture: All Action.

Designed and published by Pop Culture

POP CULTURE

RONAN FOREVER

by K. Mirza

ROLL ON RONAN

When Boyzone started out, the names Ronan and Keating meant precious little to anyone. Seen as just another try-hard in yet another boy band, the cynics laughed at him and the critics ignored him. Today, his name symbolises everything that is original in the pop universe.

So young, so fresh . . . so married. Ronan Keating, the youngest boy in the Zone, has tied the knot. But that does not mean he has divorced himself from his ever-faithful female fans, and in return their love affair with Boyzone continues in full force. As the mammoth success of Boyzone's third, and arguably finest, album continues to make and rule the waves, our Ronan's popularity is surfing new heights.

And as Ronan emerges from boy to man, even his harshest critics are being forced to realise his shelf-life is a lot longer than they expected. The swoonsome songman has proved to the fickle media that he and his band are not just a bunch of pretty faces with a "vacant" sign where the talent should be. Far from being stuck in the average "bubble-gum pop" format, they are an explosive live outfit who can write their own songs, produce dazzling performances and have more integrity and passion in their little fingers than most boy bands have all over.

With their seat in the British hall of fame secured forever, their recent victory in cracking the hallowed US market means that Boyzone now belong to the world. And it does not stop there.

While Geri Spice is busy trying to make her mark as a television presenter, Ronan has been refining his skills with more success. Ever since his appearance as one of the hosts of the 1997 Eurovision Song Contest, he has taken to the presenting game like a duck to water, making regular appearances on *Top Of The Pops* and MTV, the perfect environment for the televisual talents of the Emerald Isle's golden-boy.

Not that he is lacking in talent - a fantastic singer, dancer, lyricist and presenter, there is certainly no shortage of people who want to emulate Ronan. As well as being responsible for the legions of high-street Boyzone wannabes, Ronan has been elevated to such a level of stardom that he inspires celebrity imitators on *Stars In Their Eyes* - an honour usually reserved for musical legends.

It is all a million miles away from Ronan's musical roots in the pubs and clubs of Dublin, but like their predecessors Take That and their female equivalents The Spice Girls and All Saints, Boyzone have worked their fingers to the bone to get where they are today. And Ronan has undoubtedly accomplished more than anybody in helping to propel his band of merry boys to the fortune and glory that walks hand in hand with super-stardom.

So here's *Ronan Forever*, a book which briefly isolates Ronan from the rest of the band and gives him a thorough shake-down so you get the low-down on the most fanciable Irishman around.

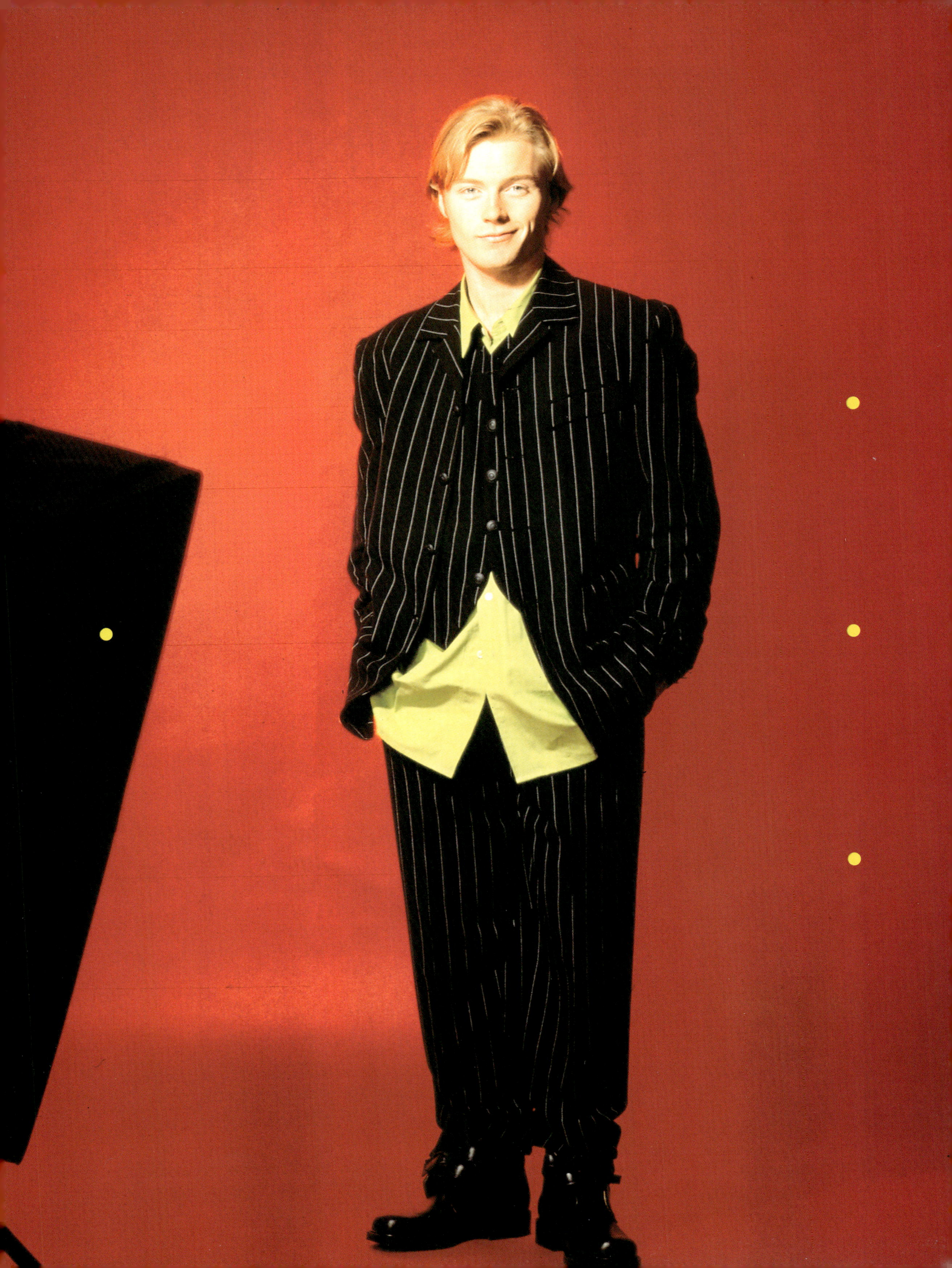

GOD'S GIFT

Step forward contestant number one - Ronan Keating. He is able to style your mum's hair, wants to be a policeman, and he makes a mean spaghetti bolognese! Oh, and boy can he sing.

Like many of the music industry's youthful success stories, Ronan Keating walked out of school without any qualifications. Despite an affinity with the English language, a passion for poetry and an artist's eye, Ronan had always felt a musical calling. He had already played the Dublin pub circuit in a couple of rock 'n' roll bands, picking up a few talent contest trophies along the way. There was also talk of Ronan accepting an educational scholarship in New York, where his brother and sister still reside, but ambition got the better of him. And when the opportunity to front Boyzone arrived, Keating knew it could be his one and only shot at the big time.

It was not an easy decision to make. He had never done anything against his mother's wishes, and when she expressed her disapproval at his dropping out of school four months before his GCSE examinations, he surprised everyone, including himself, by going against her wishes. What next - a tattoo? Yeah, he has got one of those too.

But as the sound of a million Boyzone fans rejoicing his very existence got louder and louder, those who doubted Ronan's fateful decision began to realise it was the best move he had ever made. "I believe that everything happens for a reason," he smiles. "I'm a very religious person and I think that God makes things happen." One of God's finest gifts was delivered on 3 March 1977, when Ronan Patrick John Keating was born in the Dublin suburb of Swords. Born under the star sign of Pisces, a water sign, Ronan is often indecisive, with a tendency to try his hardest to see matters from all points of view. A natural leader, he would stop bullies at school by using wit, charisma and that electric personality that makes him a winner wherever he goes. Like many of his fellow Pisceans, Ronan also has a heart full of kindness and love. The more you read about him, the more you want him. It is just too bad that he has been caught hook, line and sinker by those wedding bells!

Unlike many of his pop colleagues Ronan has never dabbled in the dangerous world of drugs and he cannot see why he should. Instead, he gets his kicks first and foremost from his music and the people who love him for it. Then there is the unstoppable passion behind his secret culinary talents, of course. One taste of his rich spaghetti bolognese, and you will see why he lives up to his reputation as a tasty dish!

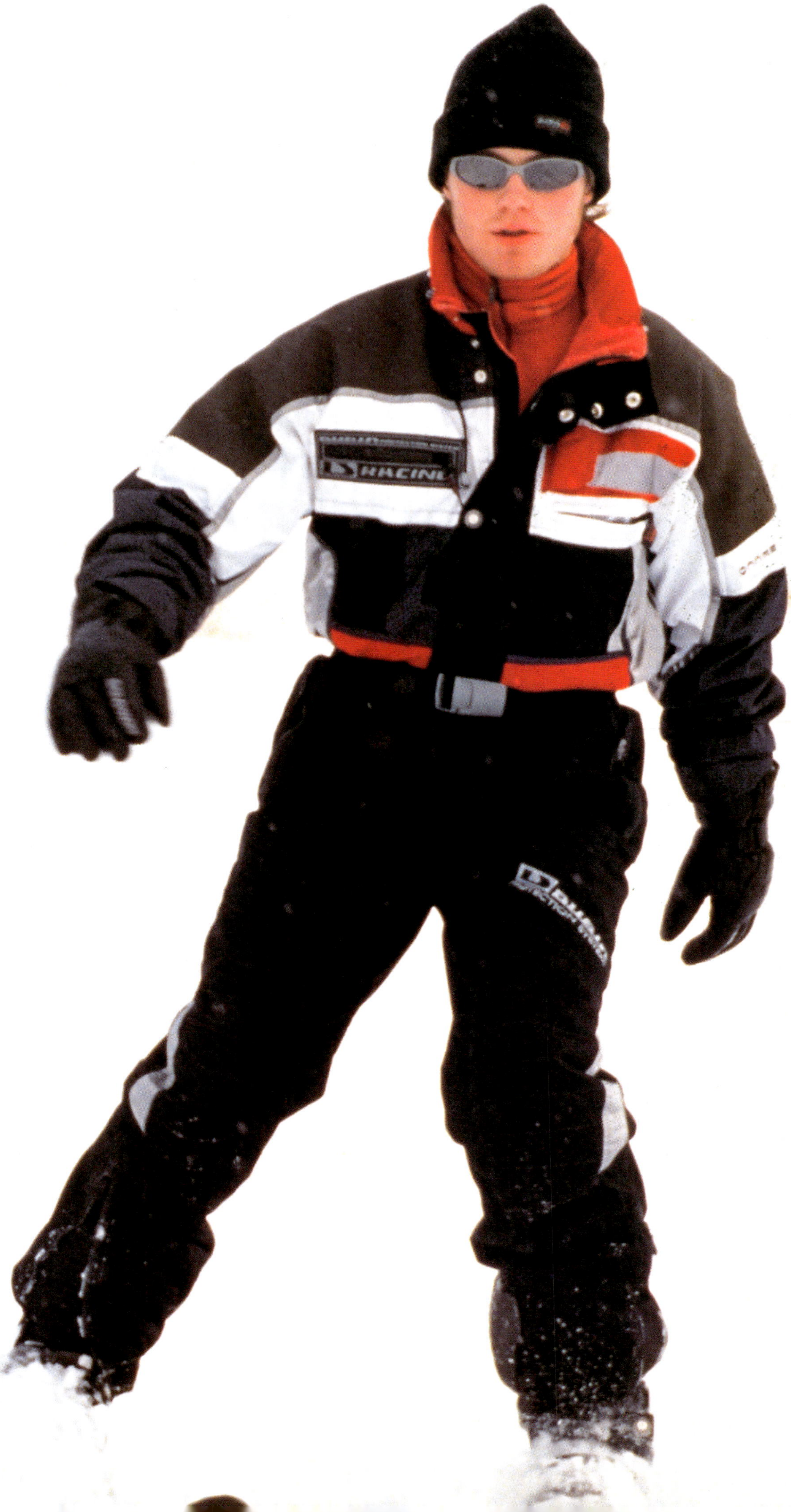

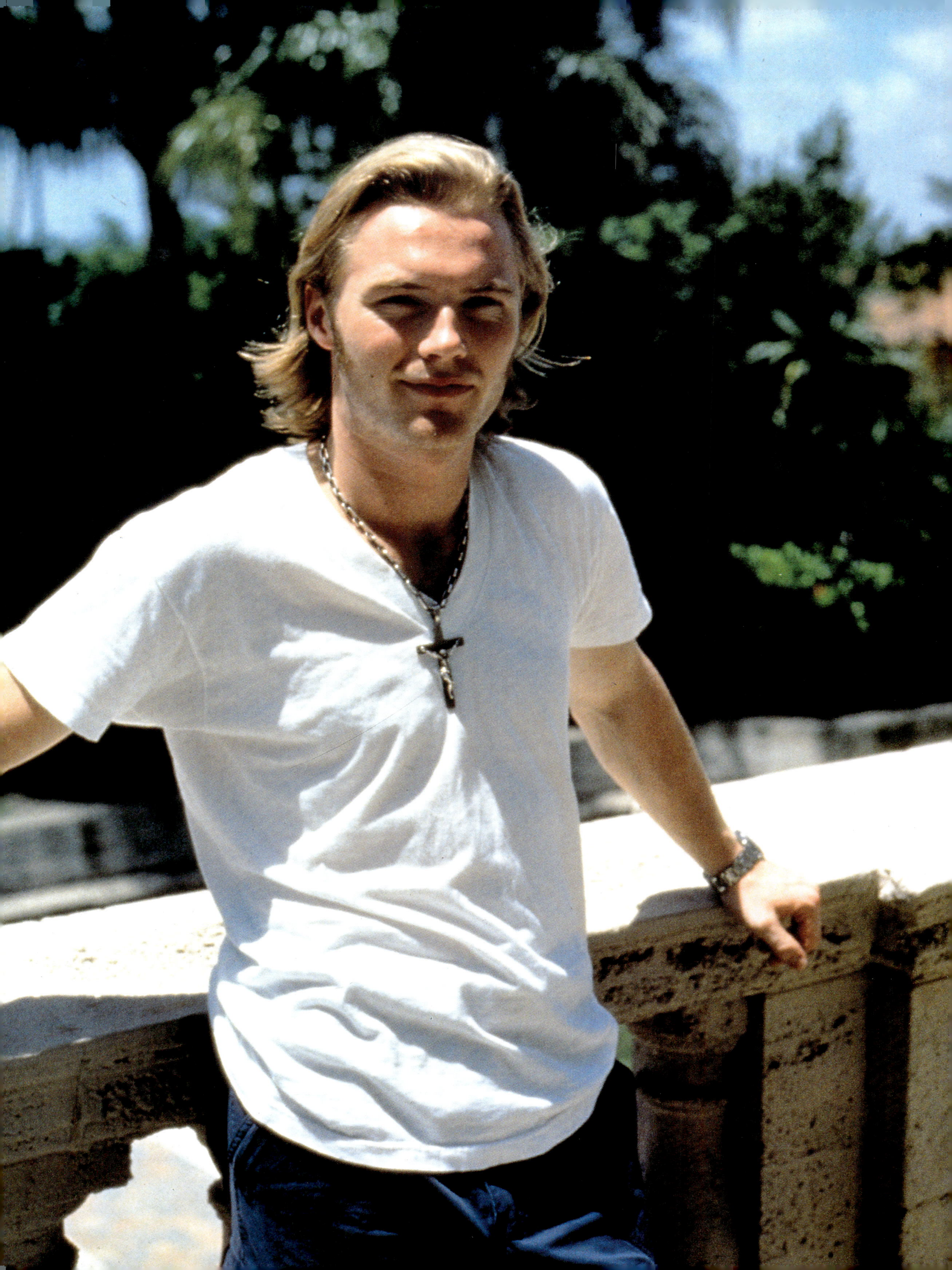

GOD'S GIFT

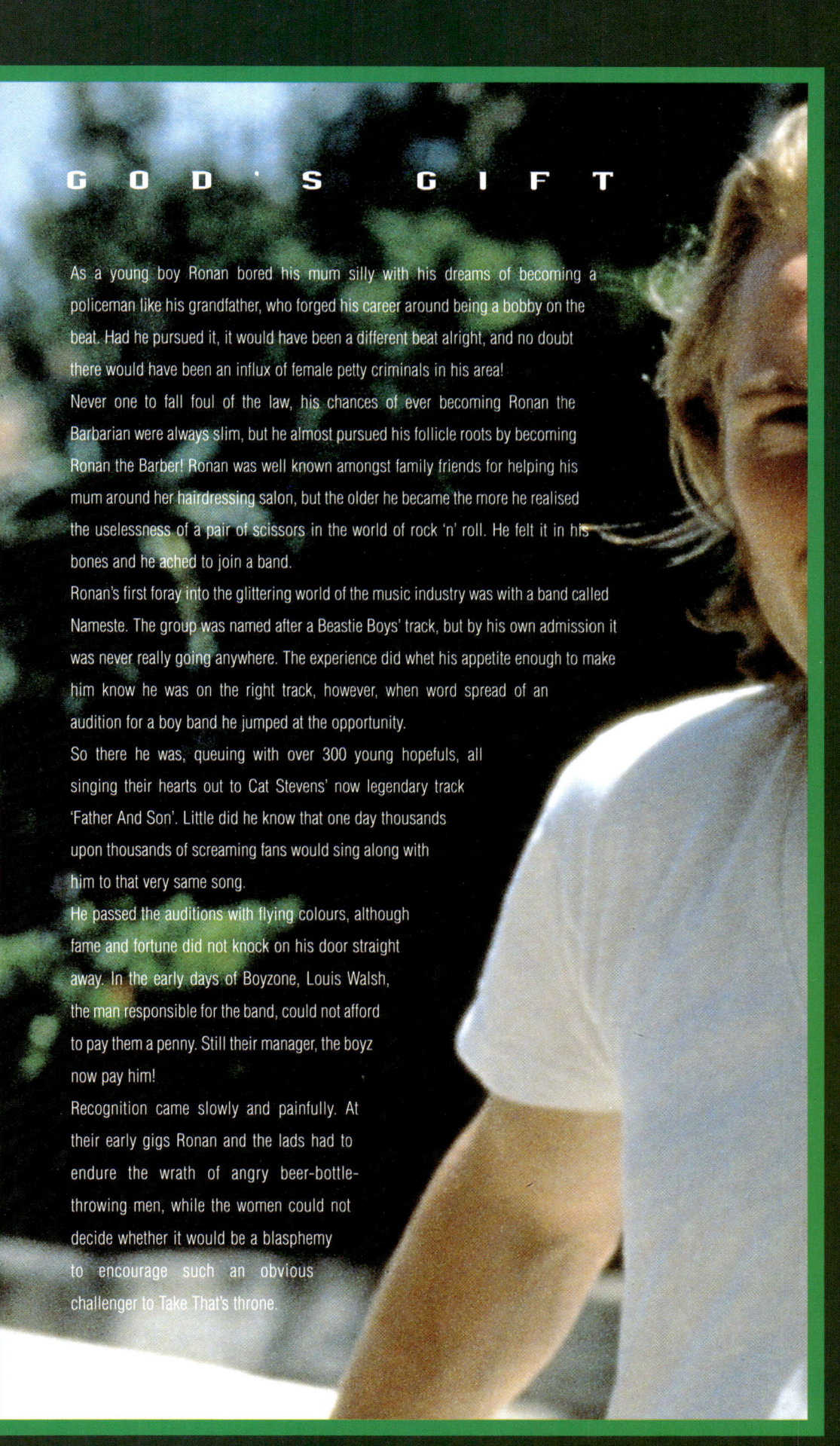

As a young boy Ronan bored his mum silly with his dreams of becoming a policeman like his grandfather, who forged his career around being a bobby on the beat. Had he pursued it, it would have been a different beat alright, and no doubt there would have been an influx of female petty criminals in his area!

Never one to fall foul of the law, his chances of ever becoming Ronan the Barbarian were always slim, but he almost pursued his follicle roots by becoming Ronan the Barber! Ronan was well known amongst family friends for helping his mum around her hairdressing salon, but the older he became the more he realised the uselessness of a pair of scissors in the world of rock 'n' roll. He felt it in his bones and he ached to join a band.

Ronan's first foray into the glittering world of the music industry was with a band called Nameste. The group was named after a Beastie Boys' track, but by his own admission it was never really going anywhere. The experience did whet his appetite enough to make him know he was on the right track, however, when word spread of an audition for a boy band he jumped at the opportunity.

So there he was, queuing with over 300 young hopefuls, all singing their hearts out to Cat Stevens' now legendary track 'Father And Son'. Little did he know that one day thousands upon thousands of screaming fans would sing along with him to that very same song.

He passed the auditions with flying colours, although fame and fortune did not knock on his door straight away. In the early days of Boyzone, Louis Walsh, the man responsible for the band, could not afford to pay them a penny. Still their manager, the boyz now pay him!

Recognition came slowly and painfully. At their early gigs Ronan and the lads had to endure the wrath of angry beer-bottle-throwing men, while the women could not decide whether it would be a blasphemy to encourage such an obvious challenger to Take That's throne.

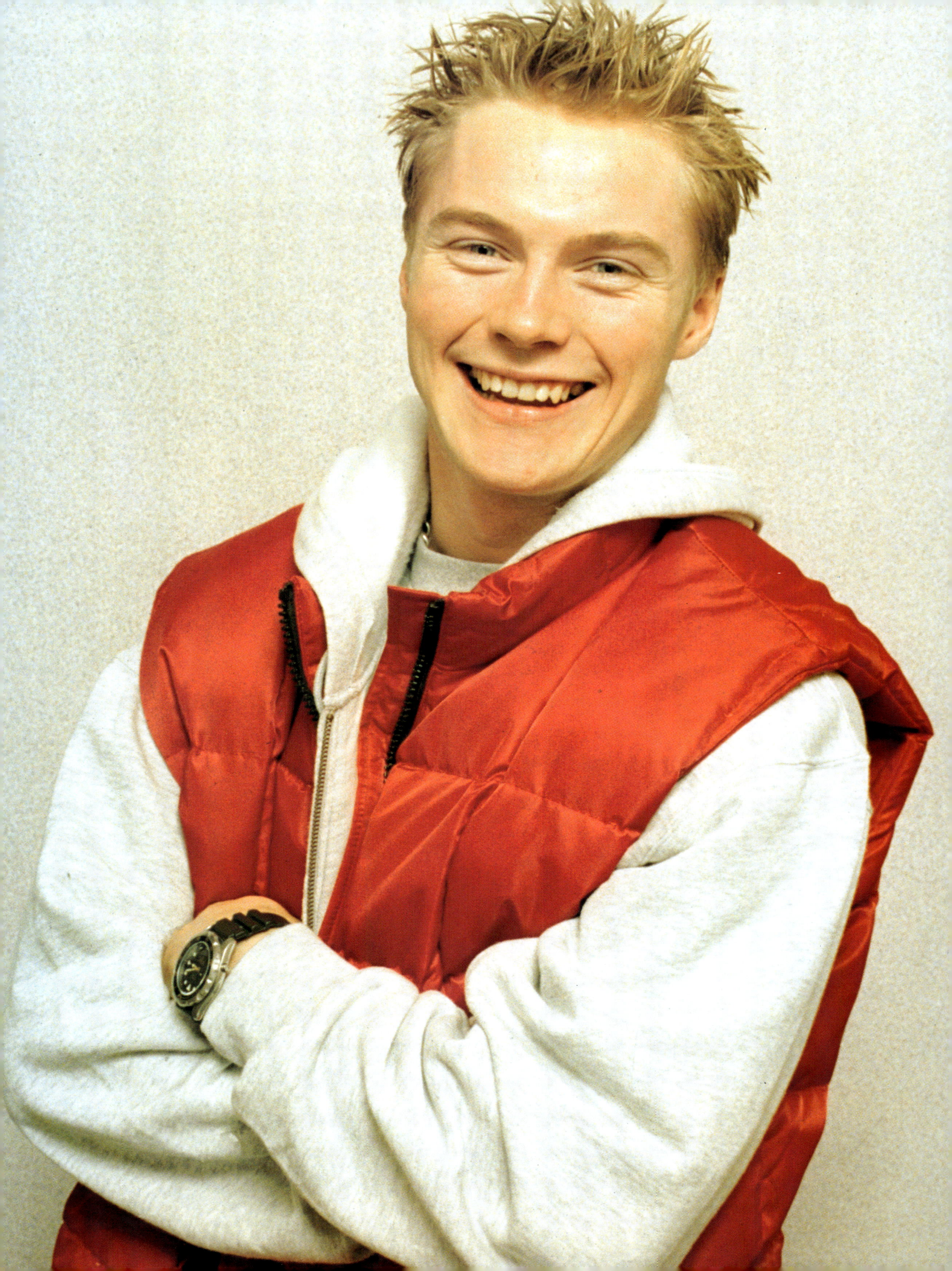

GOD'S GIFT

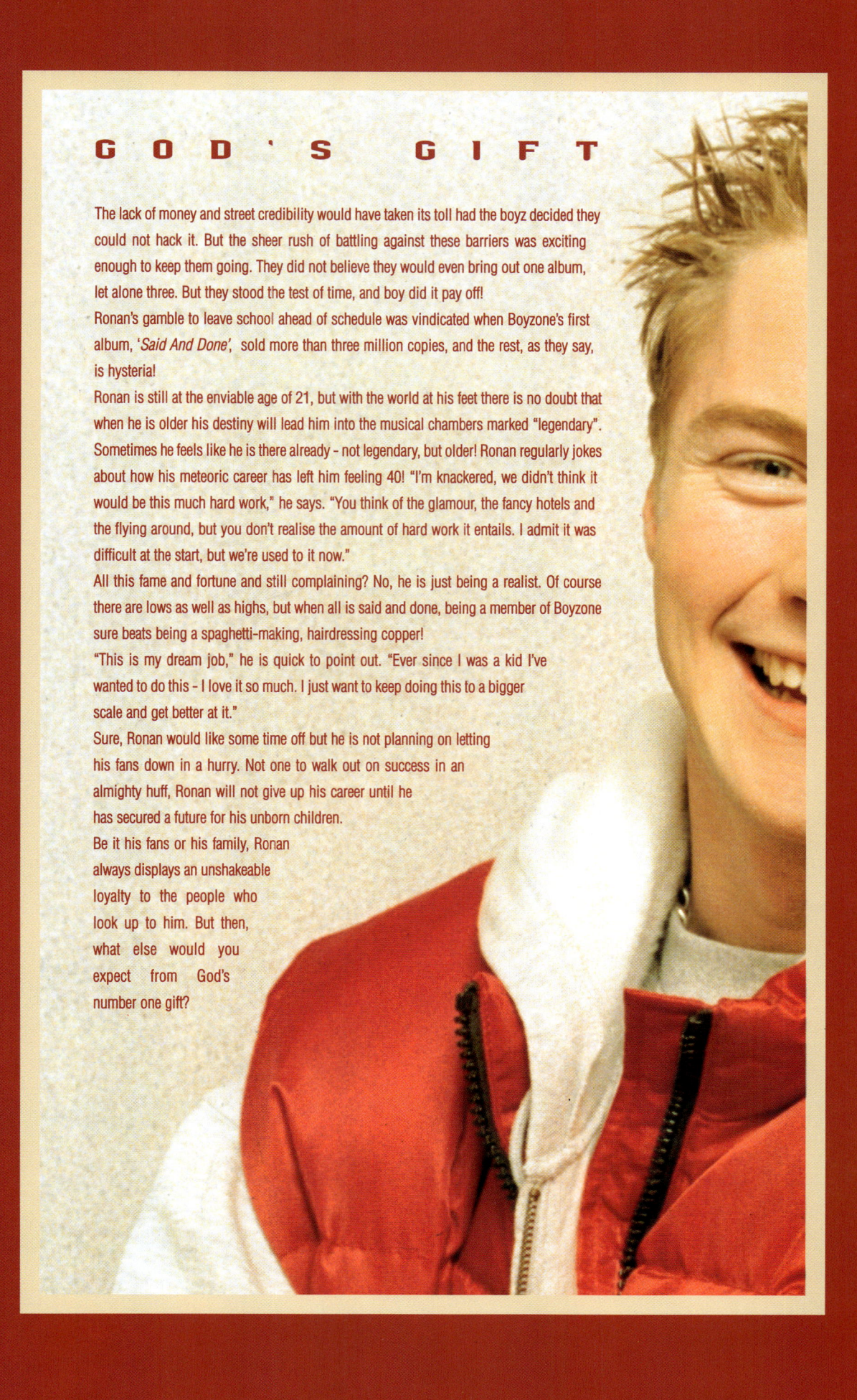

The lack of money and street credibility would have taken its toll had the boyz decided they could not hack it. But the sheer rush of battling against these barriers was exciting enough to keep them going. They did not believe they would even bring out one album, let alone three. But they stood the test of time, and boy did it pay off!

Ronan's gamble to leave school ahead of schedule was vindicated when Boyzone's first album, '*Said And Done*', sold more than three million copies, and the rest, as they say, is hysteria!

Ronan is still at the enviable age of 21, but with the world at his feet there is no doubt that when he is older his destiny will lead him into the musical chambers marked "legendary". Sometimes he feels like he is there already - not legendary, but older! Ronan regularly jokes about how his meteoric career has left him feeling 40! "I'm knackered, we didn't think it would be this much hard work," he says. "You think of the glamour, the fancy hotels and the flying around, but you don't realise the amount of hard work it entails. I admit it was difficult at the start, but we're used to it now."

All this fame and fortune and still complaining? No, he is just being a realist. Of course there are lows as well as highs, but when all is said and done, being a member of Boyzone sure beats being a spaghetti-making, hairdressing copper!

"This is my dream job," he is quick to point out. "Ever since I was a kid I've wanted to do this - I love it so much. I just want to keep doing this to a bigger scale and get better at it."

Sure, Ronan would like some time off but he is not planning on letting his fans down in a hurry. Not one to walk out on success in an almighty huff, Ronan will not give up his career until he has secured a future for his unborn children.

Be it his fans or his family, Ronan always displays an unshakeable loyalty to the people who look up to him. But then, what else would you expect from God's number one gift?

GIRLZONE

Ronan really is squeaky clean and as pure as gold . . . until Sandra Bullock comes along that is! Or Anna Friel. Or Vernie Bennett. Or Claire Danes. Or . . .

Before his marriage Ronan himself went on the record on more than one occasion claiming that he had always been saving himself for the right girl, and commenting on the state of his intact virginity. There are those who claim that the singer's remarks were nothing more than a cheap marketing ploy intended to emphasise his availability and heighten his female fan following. If that was the case then he did not make too bad a job of it, netting not only more fans but a drop-dead gorgeous wife to boot.

But Ronan is quick to dismiss the marketing accusations, reminding the public of his admirable religious beliefs. All the same, our favourite Catholic boy is still embarrassed that the whole shenanigans commanded quite so much media attention.

"The last thing I wanted to be was a Cliff Richard for the 90s," he told *The Daily Star*. "It has haunted me ever since. I wish I had never opened my mouth about it because it's all I ever get asked about!"

But Ronan had clearly taken a firm stance on the topic of sexual relationships. He has had plenty of girlfriends, and what he did with them is really no one's business but his own. He said he never went all the way, and unless you had managed to lure him up the aisle like Yvonne, you'll never know. As far as Ronan is concerned, sex and mystery go hand in hand. Even as a young boy, he could not work out the reasoning behind the male habit of boasting about sexual conquests. "I used to laugh at the kids at school who slept around," he says. "They showed no respect by wasting something so important."

Whether you think someone maintaining their virginity well past their late teens is cool or uncool is a personal matter, but that is how Ronan played it - take it or leave it. And if Ronan did leave himself pure for Yvonne, she certainly is an extremely lucky girl. There was only ever meant to be one, and she is it. Ronan readily admits that he is the faithful type who, despite being tempted by other girls whilst in a relationship, has never given in and taken advantage of the fruits on offer.

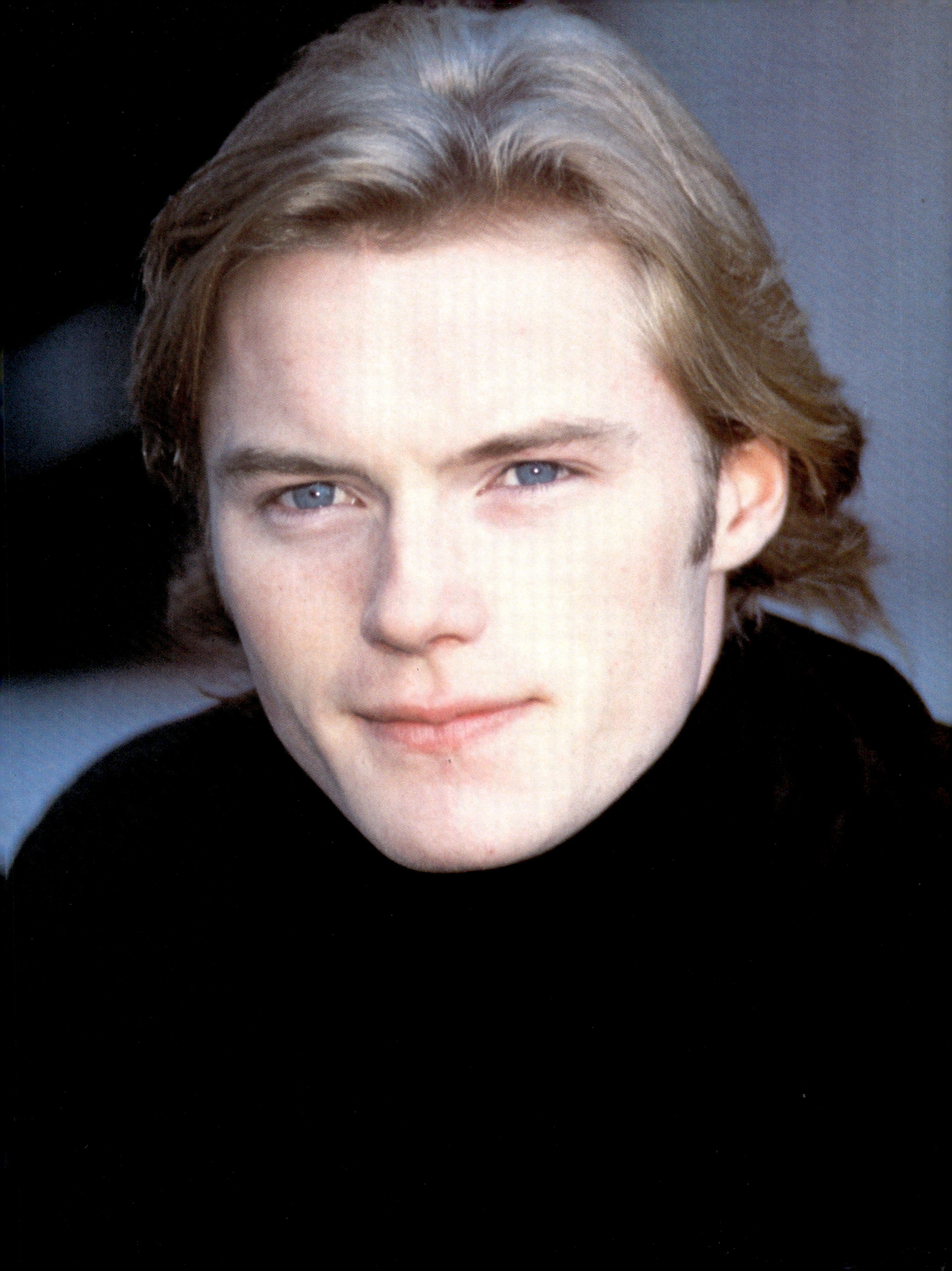

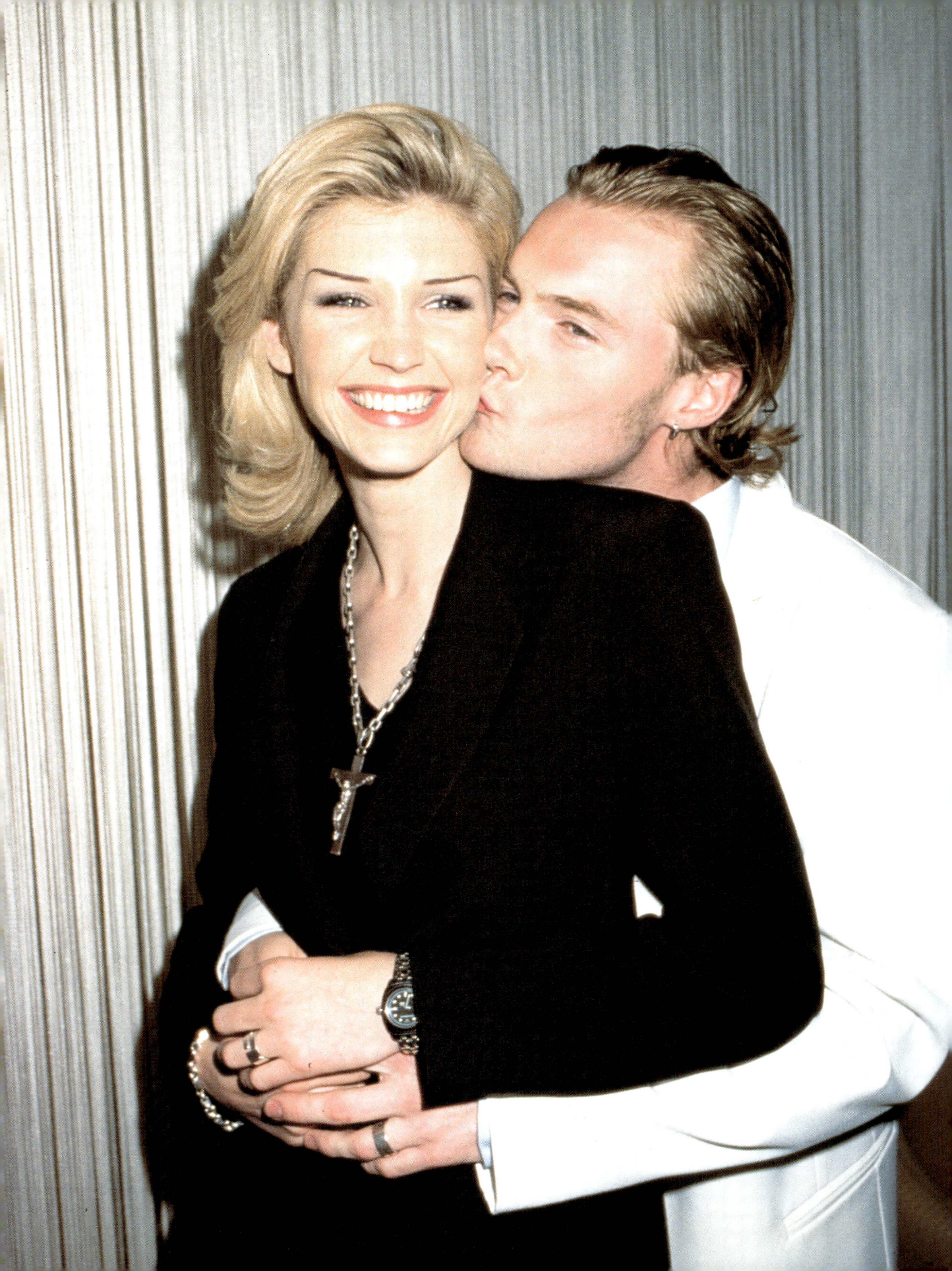

Speculation and intrigue surrounded Ronan when he was rumoured to be having a relationship with Vernie Bennett from Eternal. But in April 1997 the couple dramatically split up. The constant pressure of working in such successful bands meant they were both too rushed off their feet to have the time to sweep each other off their feet! They maintain they are still the best of friends, but after the experience Ronan promised himself he could not give his heart to someone he could only see once in a blue moon.

Ronan did not waste any time on the singles circuit, and after a matter of weeks announced to the press that he was busy wooing Claire Danes, the 17-year-old star of *William Shakespeare's Romeo And Juliet*, whom he met in a Los Angeles nightclub. Then there was MTV presenter Gabriella Martinez, who suddenly found herself mysteriously losing popularity amongst thousands of female MTV fans! I wonder why . . . ?

Ronan also confesses a mega crush on ex-*Brookside* star Anna Friel, an attraction he shares with the other members of Boyzone. Before his marriage though, Ronan was not shy of letting people know that his dream date would have been in the arms of Sandra Bullock. No doubt he has changed his tune now that he is sharing rings with Yvonne Connolly!

Yvonne truly is a stunning beauty, but that has never been the most important factor for Ronan. At the end of the day, if a girl knows how to enjoy herself and has a sense of humour, she is already good in his books. If you want to impress our Goldilocks, caking your face in the latest make-up will not work. In a nutshell, he likes his girls to look good but not be hung up on their looks. This is not to say that Ronan thinks he is Mr Perfect either. He is desperately embarrassed by his sex symbol status, and is the first to admit that his jealousy almost always gets the better of him - just ask any of his wife's fella friends! But in return, Ronan will give the right girl his half of the world. It appears there is no need for Yvonne to make an honest man of him. Sounds like Mr Keating already is, ta very much.

G I R L Z O N E

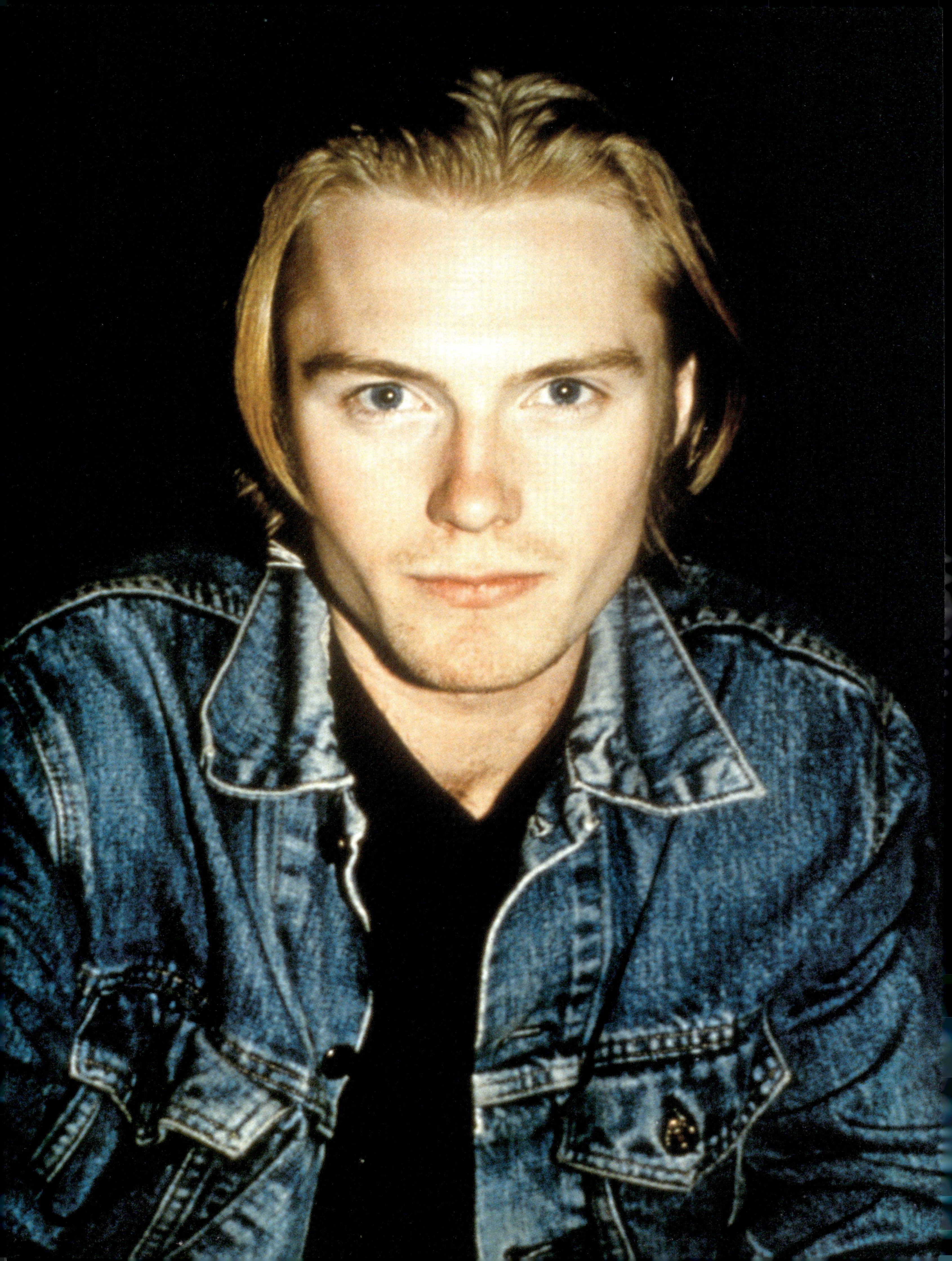

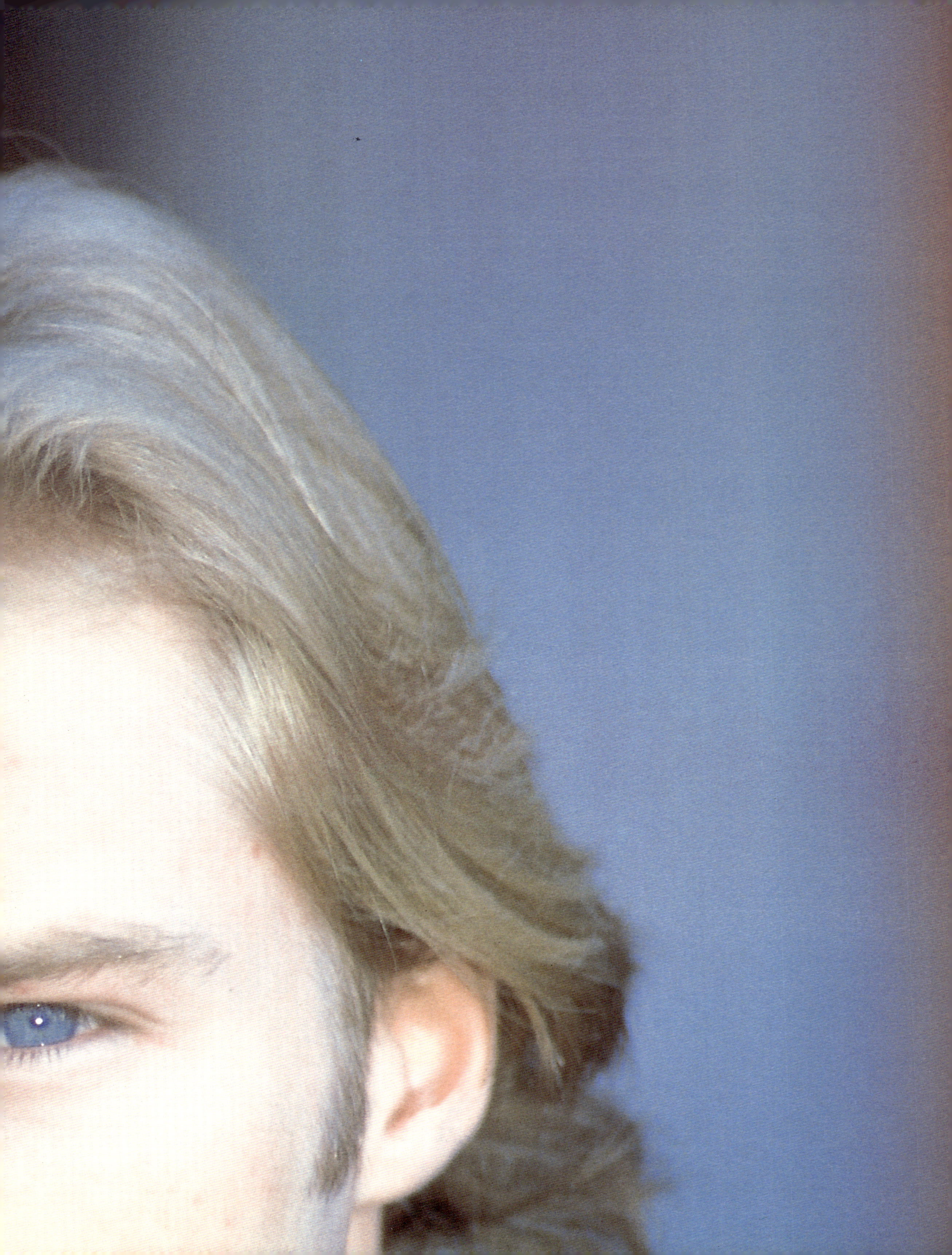

RONAN FOREVER

throb

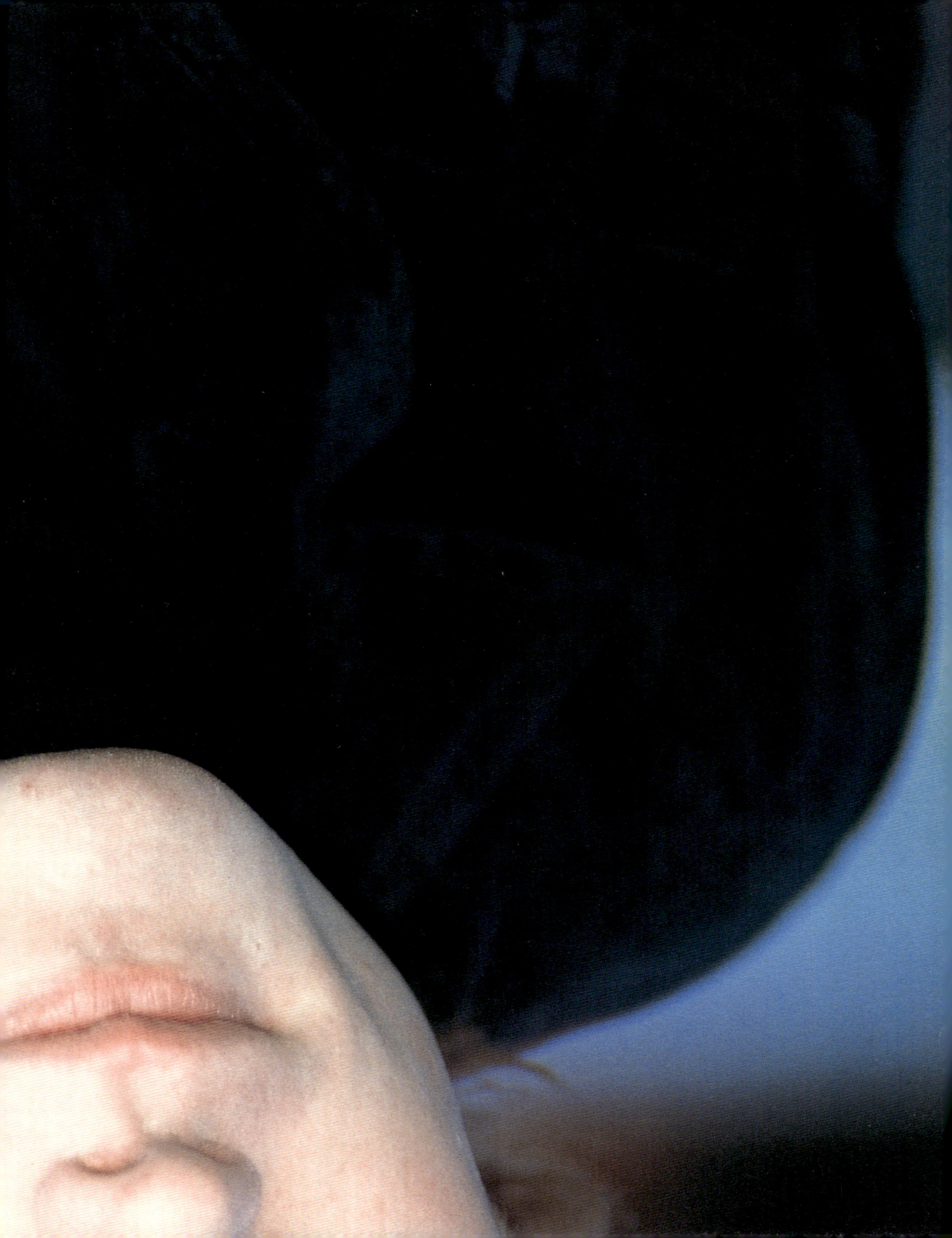

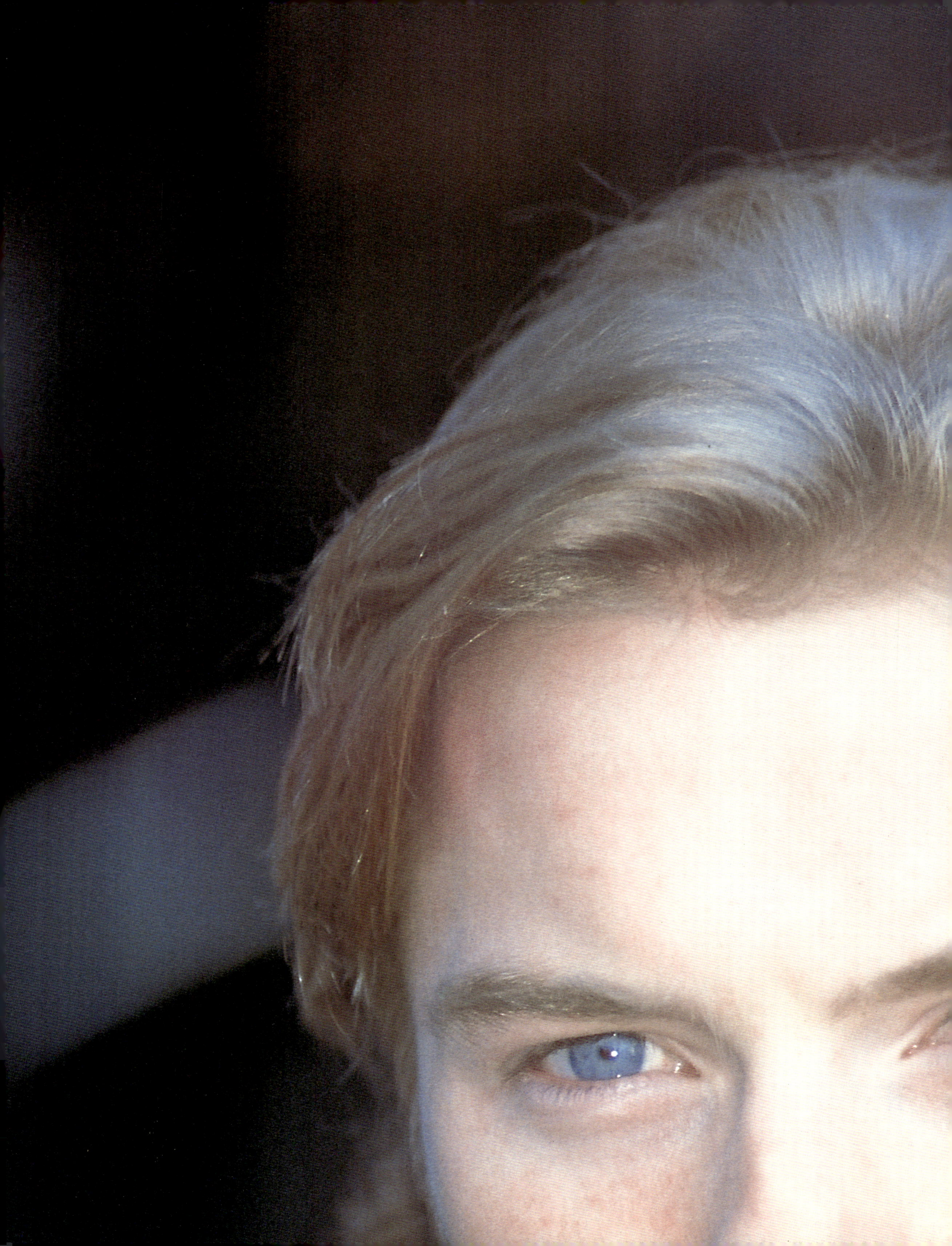

JUST ONE OF THE BOYZ

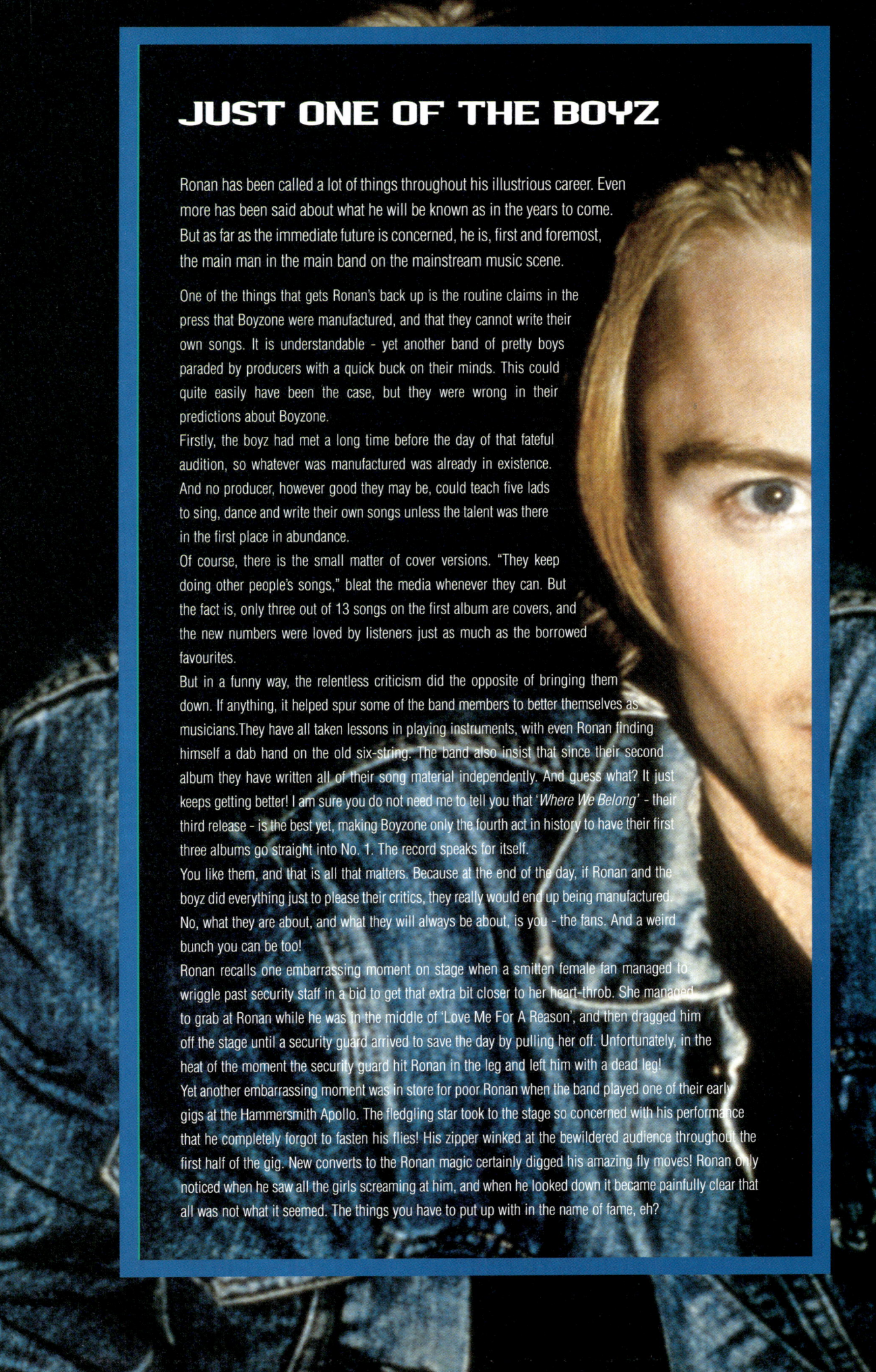

Ronan has been called a lot of things throughout his illustrious career. Even more has been said about what he will be known as in the years to come. But as far as the immediate future is concerned, he is, first and foremost, the main man in the main band on the mainstream music scene.

One of the things that gets Ronan's back up is the routine claims in the press that Boyzone were manufactured, and that they cannot write their own songs. It is understandable - yet another band of pretty boys paraded by producers with a quick buck on their minds. This could quite easily have been the case, but they were wrong in their predictions about Boyzone.

Firstly, the boyz had met a long time before the day of that fateful audition, so whatever was manufactured was already in existence. And no producer, however good they may be, could teach five lads to sing, dance and write their own songs unless the talent was there in the first place in abundance.

Of course, there is the small matter of cover versions. "They keep doing other people's songs," bleat the media whenever they can. But the fact is, only three out of 13 songs on the first album are covers, and the new numbers were loved by listeners just as much as the borrowed favourites.

But in a funny way, the relentless criticism did the opposite of bringing them down. If anything, it helped spur some of the band members to better themselves as musicians. They have all taken lessons in playing instruments, with even Ronan finding himself a dab hand on the old six-string. The band also insist that since their second album they have written all of their song material independently. And guess what? It just keeps getting better! I am sure you do not need me to tell you that *Where We Belong* - their third release - is the best yet, making Boyzone only the fourth act in history to have their first three albums go straight into No. 1. The record speaks for itself.

You like them, and that is all that matters. Because at the end of the day, if Ronan and the boyz did everything just to please their critics, they really would end up being manufactured. No, what they are about, and what they will always be about, is you - the fans. And a weird bunch you can be too!

Ronan recalls one embarrassing moment on stage when a smitten female fan managed to wriggle past security staff in a bid to get that extra bit closer to her heart-throb. She managed to grab at Ronan while he was in the middle of 'Love Me For A Reason', and then dragged him off the stage until a security guard arrived to save the day by pulling her off. Unfortunately, in the heat of the moment the security guard hit Ronan in the leg and left him with a dead leg!

Yet another embarrassing moment was in store for poor Ronan when the band played one of their early gigs at the Hammersmith Apollo. The fledgling star took to the stage so concerned with his performance that he completely forgot to fasten his flies! His zipper winked at the bewildered audience throughout the first half of the gig. New converts to the Ronan magic certainly digged his amazing fly moves! Ronan only noticed when he saw all the girls screaming at him, and when he looked down it became painfully clear that all was not what it seemed. The things you have to put up with in the name of fame, eh?

JUST ONE OF THE BOYZ

But it is not just embarrassing episodes that Ronan has to worry about. All pop stars have to face the future and wonder if the road they are following will continue as smoothly as it has been, or whether a drastic change in direction will be called for. After all, on the pop path anything can happen.

Hearts stopped the world over one cold day in February 1997 when reports that Ronan and the rest of the band were in a plane crash. The news monopolised the front pages of the papers. As luck would have it, they narrowly cheated death after the engine failed on the plane that was carrying them to a promotional campaign in Australia. Luckily the adept pilot managed to crash land the plane in the Antipodean desert, and apart from a few cuts and bruises the group walked away with their lives intact. A miraculous escape; it seems God was looking after his gifts that day. And Ronan, who admits that it was one of the scariest experiences of his life, thought the time to meet his maker had arrived sooner than expected.

But even that experience does not come close to his two major fears in life - snakes are the first and the other is life after Boyzone. That scares us more than it does him, however. It goes without saying that everyone believes Ronan will pursue a successful solo career once Boyzone come to their natural end. The million dollar question is - when? Any record company worth their salt would snap Ronan up if he were to announce that he was going solo, but judging by the tone of his interviews and the amount of fun he is having with his brethren, that option is still light-years away. Right now the band are riding higher in the hearts of their global fan base than ever before. Keating hopes that the band will emulate Wet Wet Wet who have managed to progress from strength to strength. Let us just keep putting pennies in the wishing well and hope that wish comes true.

There is no way anyone can disguise Ronan Keating's ambition. He and Steve have already been approached to make movies, and with a Spice Girls-style film project already in the pipeline, it will not be long before Ewan McGregor has a rival. But acting would always be a luxury, and Ronan's soul will remain on the musical stage. If he one day succeeds in launching a record-breaking solo career like his hero George Michael, he would rest a happy man.

So even if the unthinkable happens and Boyzone announce that dreaded split, rest assured, Ronan is not going to be leaving us in a hurry.

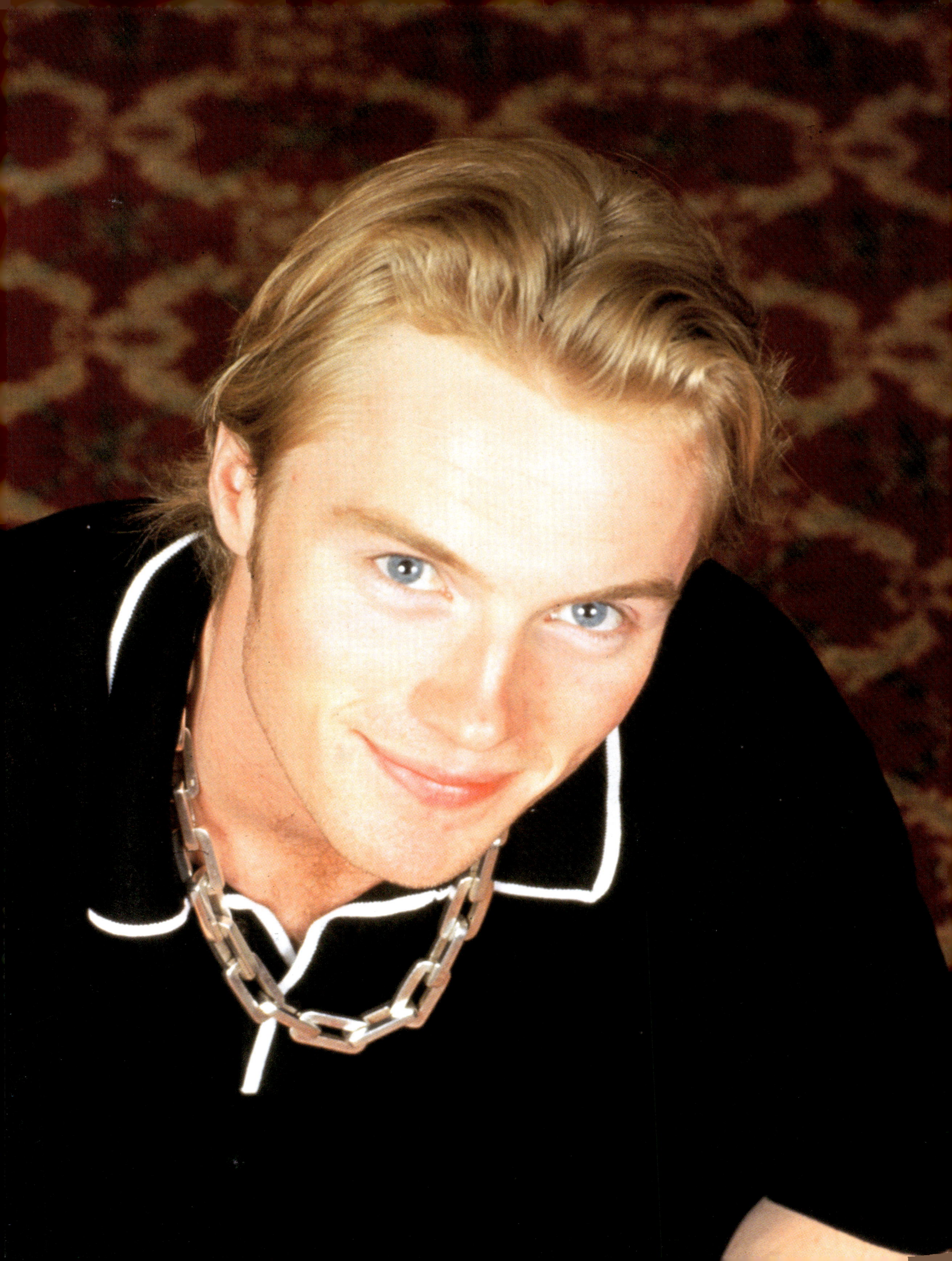

RONAN THE CONQUEROR

Journalists can exhaust the dictionary trying to pin-point the right words to describe our babelicious, scrumptious funky hunk. But no one word fits better than a simple "phwoooar"...

So what makes Ronan the hottest member of Boyzone? It is pretty simple. Just about every one of Ronan's features, both physical and personal, place him head and shoulders above the others. Sure, Stephen Gately has a cute smile and floppy hair. OK, Keith Duffy may have been blessed with eyes that melt hearts like ice-cream. Yes, Shane Lynch has the kind of body that Peter Andre would kill for; and so what if Mikey Graham is the most sophisticated dude since the dawn of time? Ronan Keating still wins hands down.

He has got it all. Those winning boy-next-door looks, the cool, understated personality, refreshing sincerity, enviable honesty and a smile that can turn you into a grinning mess! And unlike his previous competitor Gary Barlow (put them dancing shoes away, boyo!), he is a tip-top footworker, well known for busting the funkiest of moves. His singing ability is unparalleled (despite the fact that he was fired by the school choir!), and his eye for street style makes his band as far away from try-hard territory as the Backstreet Boys are from the back door!

None of this means that the other four are not brilliant. It just means Ronan is that little bit better than brilliant. And the other four are all clever lads - they must know when they're beaten!

Perhaps his best-loved feature are those mesmeric deep blue eyes. When he blushes, the female world swoons. When he smiles, and he does so with reassuring regularity, his entire face lights up and his contentment becomes simply contagious. It is almost impossible to resist a grin like that. If smiling was an Olympic event, Ronan would walk away with the gold medal every time.

But it is not just the looks. His drive is a feat in itself. While many big-mouthed rock stars drop out of tours because of the slightest hangover, Ronan always puts his work first. In 1996 he defied his doctor's orders to cancel a gig in Birmingham despite suffering from acute bronchitis. If he let his fans down, for whatever reason, he would not be able to look them in the eye.

But charming as those Irish eyes are, they are extremely effective at masking whatever goes on inside the elusive Ronan Keating's head. He is our international man of mystery and wears the word "enigma" like a cloak around his persona.

There are some things about the man we will just never know. And that makes him all the more alluring!

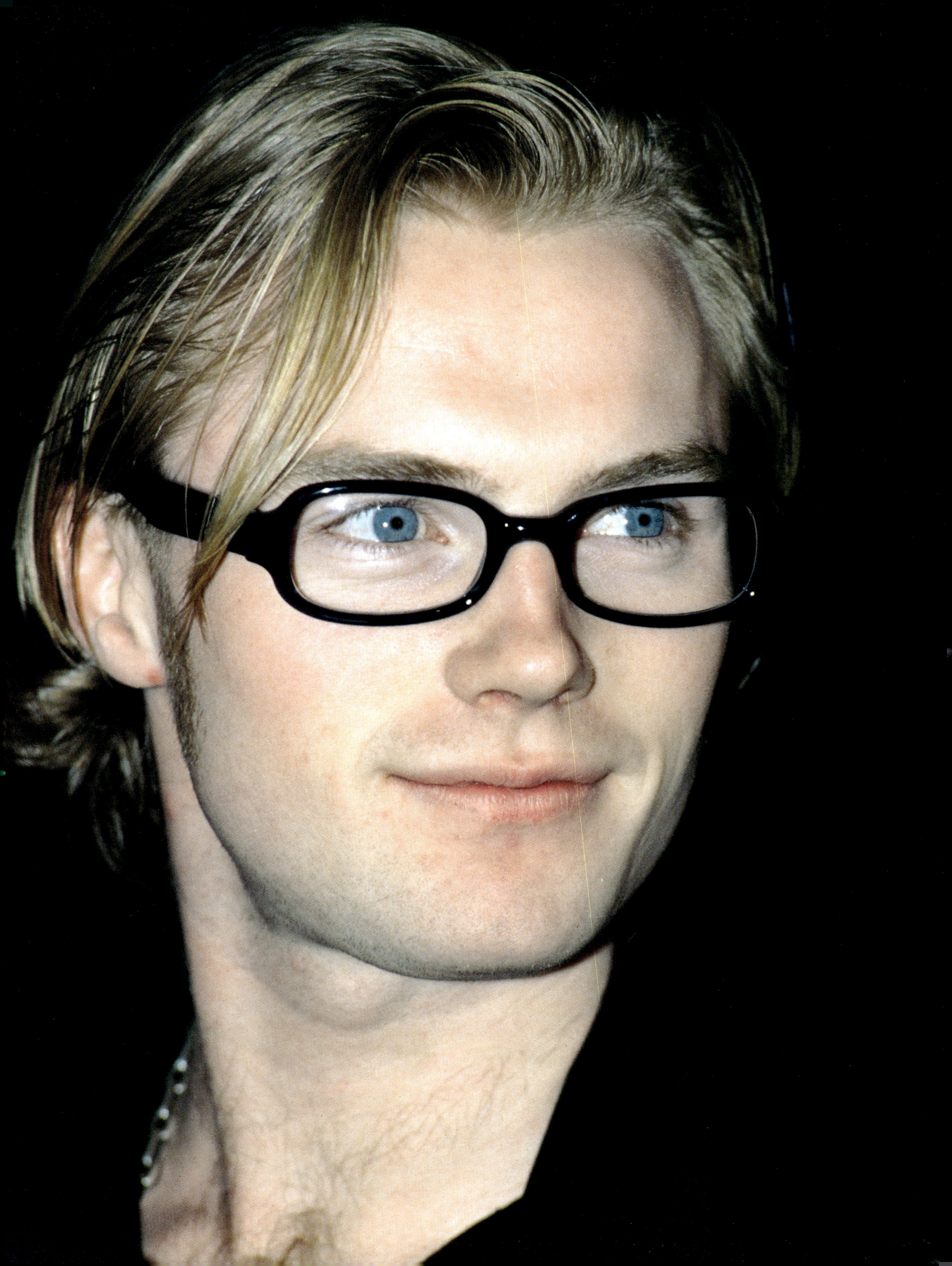

RONAN THE CONQUERER

But then, what we do know about Ronan is that he lives life the way he wants to. When it is time to rock 'n' roll, he will live in the fast lane like the best of them. And when it comes to chilling, he is not afraid to bring out the slippers and armchair either! He likes nothing better than to spend a rare day off driving fast cars with Shane. Then, at the other end of the recreational barometer, he adores lounging around his home in tatty old comfort clothes reading a good book. He may be the leading figure in one of the country's hottest bands, but out of the spotlight Ronan's shy and retiring side is one of the music industry's best kept secrets. Someone once commented that Ronan looks like an angel and sings like the devil, a fascinating combination if ever there was one. People who know Ronan closely claim that he can pretend to be a tough guy but deep down he is really a pussycat.

As early as 1996, Ronan was voted the country's most fanciable man in one of the country's leading teen magazines. At first he was afraid that his mates would subject him to a barrage of abuse, but was relieved when they suggested he put the award next to his trophies for Best Haircut and Best Male Spectacle Wearer! A pretty head he may have, but a big head he certainly has not. Still in constant touch with his old buddies, Ronan always hooks up with them in the same place they used to meet before his glory days _ a club that is now famous because of certain auditions that were held there a few years ago. That's right, he always makes a beeline for The POD. He is a bit of a party animal and loves nothing more than a night of hardcore clubbing with his old friends. Everyone treats him just as they used to, and if anybody tries to start trouble with the unassuming Ronan, his old mates always run to the rescue, defusing any potential fights with the wit and charm which have evidently rubbed off on their young friend. Even if things get a little hairy and Ronan is forced to make a dash for it, he could probably out-run most opponents seeing as he was an athletics champion in his school days.

However, his best friends are still the members of the band. While groups like Take That and The Spice Girls suffered a fatal division because of internal fighting which resulted in key members storming out, there is little chance that Boyzone will ever fall out.

And whether they are touring on the road or just cruising it for the buzz, Ronan makes sure they are having a laugh. When they were all back home together he indulged in his passion for racing and hired *Kart City* in Dublin. And even though it was Shane, the man reputed for having no fear, who walked away with the day's prize, Ronan was more than happy to come second to a best mate.

But the hardest test was just around the corner, and Ronan found himself slap bang in the middle of it.

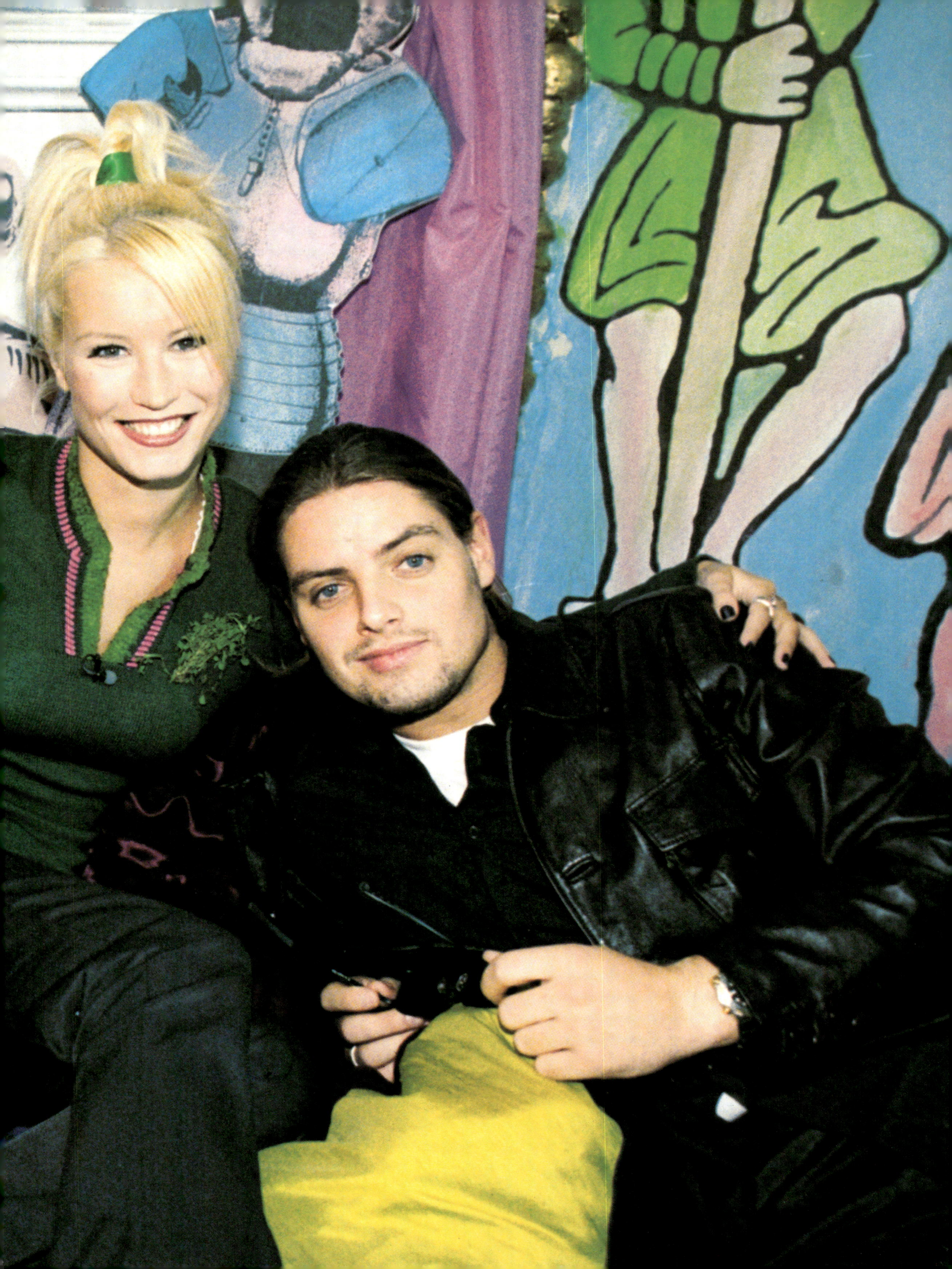

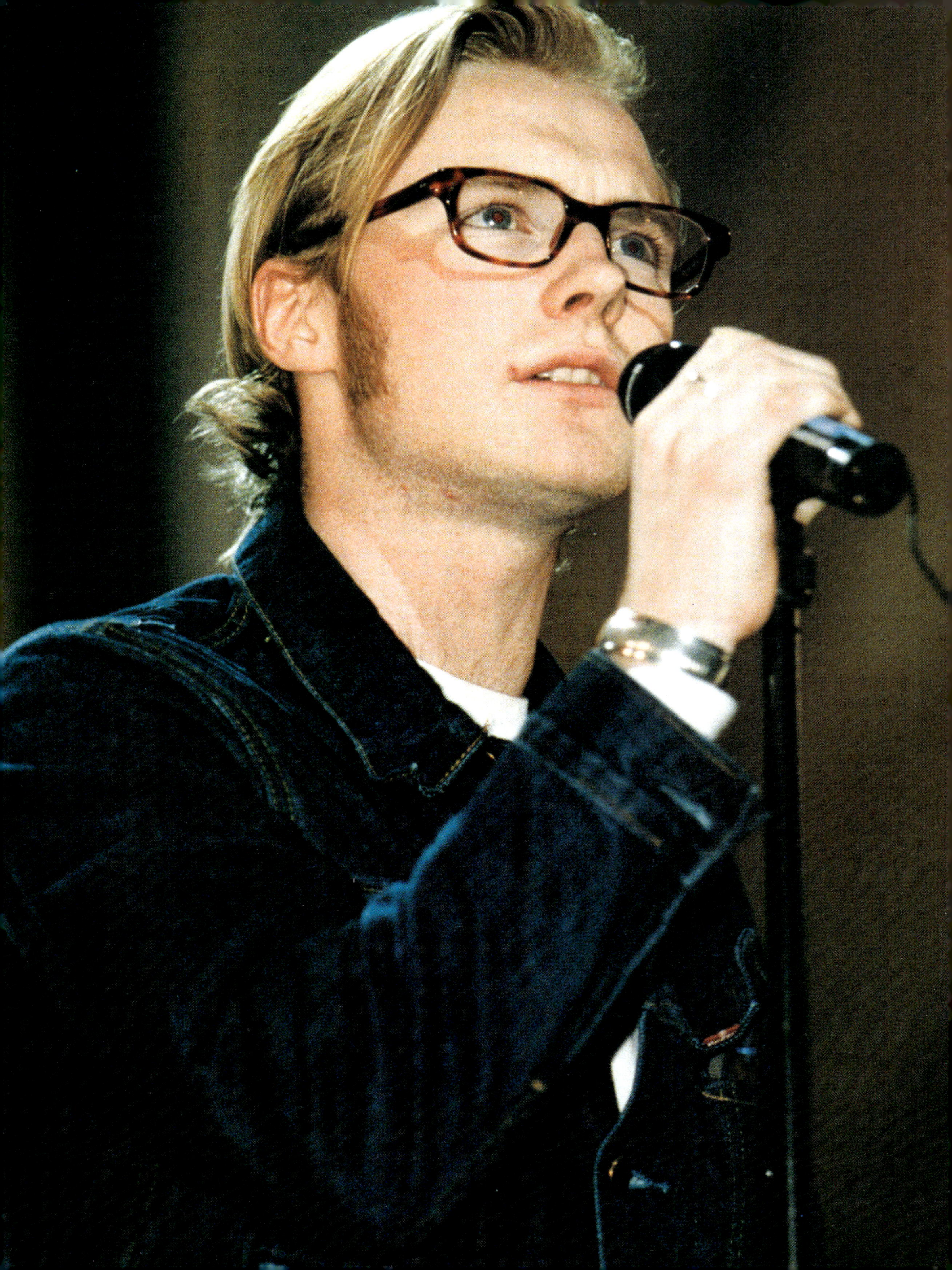

TWILIGHT ZONE

Suddenly, when it looked as though nothing could go wrong in Ronan's life, everything did. His mum, his gran and his cousin all died within the space of two months. Things had never looked so bleak . . .

This was weird city. Ronan was fully prepared for the pitfalls of fame - a record misfiring in the charts he could handle, a gig that did not sell-out he could live with, a bad review would just be a matter of course - but to deal with not one but three losses close to him, and having to grieve for them publicly? Nothing could have prepared him for that. It is fair to say they were the darkest days of his life. What good is a No.1 record when your mum is not there to be proud of it? She was everything to him, and everything he did, he did for her. When he had cracked the incredibly difficult US market, the first person he rang to rejoice with was . . . yes, his mum.

So there he was in New York, cementing the group's success with sell-out tours, when the phone rang. It was not his then girlfriend Gabriella Martinez who was expecting him at Mexico City for a wild weekend. It was that call. The call he never wanted to take.

His mother had been suffering from breast cancer, and as far as Ronan knew the operation she underwent the year before followed by the painful chemotherapy treatment had meant she would be alright. The pain and suffering was over for good. Even the night before 51-year-old Marie Keating passed away, Ronan had a dream in which he and his sister were sitting beside his mother, dressed in gold, with her whispering: "It's OK. I'm happy now. Please let me go."

The phone call only confirmed that his worst dream was coming true. It was a nurse informing him that his mother had taken a turn for the worse. He was on the first plane back to County Kildare, where Marie Keating was refusing to leave this earth without taking one last gaze at her favourite little boy. Marie Keating died a happy and a very proud woman.

But Ronan had just lost a best friend, an anchor, a mother and the woman he called "the only one that really counts." She was the one person who helped him keep his head above the water of fame. "Every time I go home my mum sends me out to get the groceries. She makes sure that I don't get too big headed," he used to say.

The days which followed made no sense to Ronan, and held even less justice. Fate has a terrible habit of handing a bad deal to someone who is already down, and the hand Ronan received next contained jokers with all the charm of Pennywise the clown from Stephen King's *IT*!

His mother's last breaths were still fresh in the air when his beloved grandmother Annie died. Never at a loss for words when it comes to expressing himself through song, Ronan could say nothing more than: "I have been walking around like a zombie. There is a massive gap in my life, a huge void."

It was a void that only widened when, out of the blue, his 16-year-old cousin Laurinda Clarke contracted meningitis and passed away. Ronan was understandably on the verge of an almighty nervous breakdown, and had he decided to hang up his boots and quit there and then, who could have blamed him?

He now found himself questioning the one thing that had kept him strong throughout his life - his faith in God. Suddenly, everything he stood for had been completely shaken up. But when he came to his senses, realising his mother had gone to a peaceful place and would always be around to watch over him, Ronan went back to doing what his mother would have expected him to do.

And with the faith of the people around him, he bounced back stronger than before. Without his fans, family and friends, he might just have lost the will to survive. He did not. And a million people stood by him. Ronan will one day pen a song in the memory of his losses, particularly his mother, but until then there is a job to be done.

In the face of all this tragedy, Ronan Keating is still an entertainer. His mum would be have been so proud.

BRIDE AND JOY

The two favourite words of a female Boyzone fan are certainly not Yvonne Connolly. But when you realise how much she means to the man you love, you will thank her for taking Ronan back into the joyzone.

Every cloud has a silver lining, and Ronan found a rainbow at the end of his . . . complete with a pot of gold. Step forward the beautiful model Yvonne Connolly. She has had her eye on him since she was 13 and he was just 10 years old, and similarly all the men she has ever known have had their eyes on her. The two drifted apart as kids do, but a chance meeting two years ago reminded the pair of the joy that closeness can bring.

It hit Ronan from nowhere one day. They were very close friends, telling each other everything that could possibly be said about themselves, when he realised he felt the need for just that little bit more. He kept his thoughts to himself for a very long time, fearing that any admission of his feelings might seriously jeopardise their platonic union, but eventually that was the price he was prepared to pay.

As luck would have it, Yvonne had been harbouring a little secret of her own. All the time she was dating some of the most eligible bachelors in town, she really knew there was only ever one guy for her - her best friend, her little Tin Tin, her very own boy - her Mr Keating.

It is the stuff of Shakespearean romances, except that unlike Romeo and Juliet, romance followed tragedy instead of the other way round! And not even the most ardent female fan could be bitter at Yvonne's fairytale catch. She was there for him during the worst patch of his life, and helped him come out the other end with a smile on his face.

And all those hours we spent wondering whether he really is a virgin or not can finally come to an end. All that waiting for the right girl to come along was suddenly over, because there she was all along, right in front of his eyes . . . Yvonne Connolly. It was certainly unexpected. There they were, Yvonne helping Ronan lick his wounds over a game of golf on a Caribbean island, when he took the bravest shot he ever attempted. Ronan sank the ball, popped the question, and by the 18th hole he had well and truly bagged his birdie!

Before you could say "Bob's your uncle", Ronan's brother Gary jetted over to act as a witness, while an 83-year-old judge conducted the quiet but idyllic ceremony. The whole process was far from the typically lavish affair that most pop stars are accustomed to, but Ronan knew full well that he was breaking a lot of young hearts by tying the knot. There was no point rubbing their noses in it with a million dollar bash, something that would no doubt be publicised everywhere in the world. He respected his fans' feelings, and in return his fans have not left him, even though they now know they can never have him all to themselves.

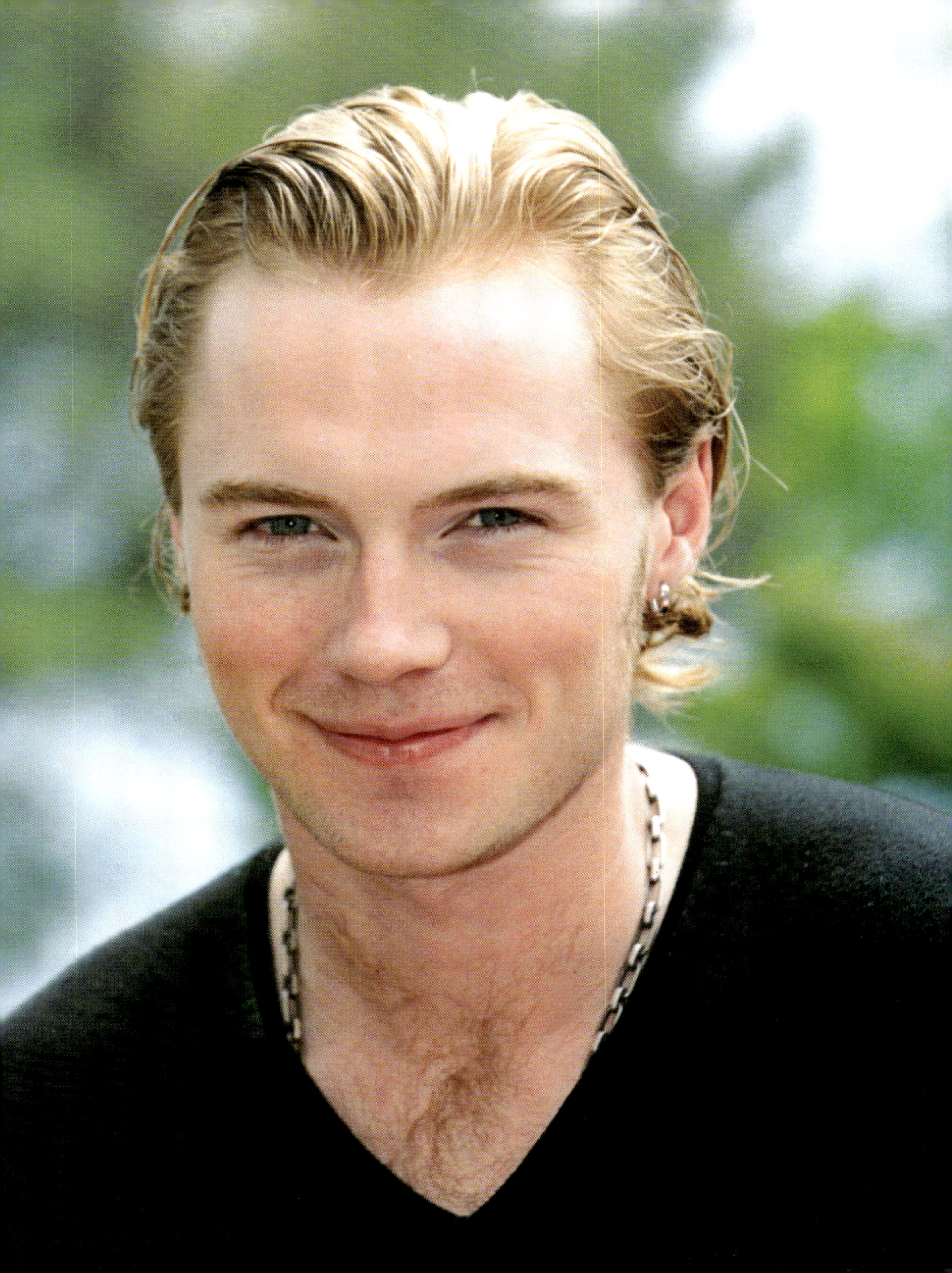

BRIDE AND JOY

Fans aside, there were of course other things to consider. From a personal point of view, Ronan did not want to get bogged down by contradictory advice from people around him. Some would have said it was too big a move to make too soon, and that he should wait until he had fully come to terms with his mother's death. Others would have pointed out that a marriage might deal a severe blow to his fan base, and that there was no harm waiting a little while longer. Some might even have suggested that he was just using Yvonne to get over his grief. Ronan did not want to hear any of that. As far as he was concerned, he had made the right decision. The only person he double checked with was his best man, his brother Gary, and Gary gave him the reassuring green light.

But all this concern over the reaction of his fans, friends and family did not mean Ronan dithered when it came to sweeping Yvonne off her feet. After a magical honeymoon in New York, where Ronan no doubt exorcised his virginity once and for all, his wife officially became the only woman in his life when he dedicated a tribute to her at the *World Music Awards* in Monte Carlo.

After years of proclaiming that his mother was his number one gal, Yvonne did feel uneasy about filling her shoes. But Ronan assured her that she was not a replacement. It was what destiny had chosen for them. It was what his mother would have wanted. "Mam knew Yvonne and liked her and, in a way, I believe she set this up," he said in a frank interview with *The Daily Mail*, adding: "She would have wanted this to be the next step in my life."

But far from just filling in the holes in Ronan's life by becoming plain old Mrs Keating, Yvonne is set to take her modelling career further, where only angels dare to catwalk. And guess who she is walking up the fashion aisles with?

Yep, the blonde duo are set to become the hottest toasts of the fashion world, with a five-figure deal to model for the incredibly swish designer John Rocha later this year. And that, believe it or not, is cheap!

Experts are saying that they are only being paid in the thousands because Ronan and Rocha go way back, and warn any other designers that they will have to buy new elastic to stretch their budgets if they want the couple on board. None of which means Ronan the catwalker will overtake Ronan the singer. He has been offered modelling and acting jobs by the bucket-load since day one, and while he will pursue both avenues of opportunity to a certain extent, music will remain his first love. That is what got him where he is today - and he will never turn his back on anything or anyone that helped hoist him up there.

And today, from the top of the world, he can only say thank you.

RONAN ON AND ON

Musician, actor, presenter, model and all-round nice guy. Is there no stopping the irresistible force of Ronan Keating? You will have better luck trying to stop a tidal wave.

It has been a long time since Ronan donned the standard boy band wide-collar white shirt to first perform 'Stay' on *Top Of The Pops*, and at 21 he is more mature, wise and, in his own way, wilder. Just ask the punters who were at his 21st birthday bash. You could not get him away from the shandy for love nor money!

Of course he is just that bit more subdued than he used to be, understandable in the face of recent events, but even when he is quiet he is still the king of cool! Despite the lows, the rise and rise of Ronan just keeps spiralling, without any danger of ever getting out of control.

He has been through the worst of it. When stardom hits too early, too many fall prey to its temptations. Some turn to drink and drugs, some get such an inflated ego that their head literally explodes, while others blow it all, lose it all, and whimper off into oblivion.

Ronan has done his five-year stretch at the sex, drugs and rock 'n' roll initiation ceremony and has come out untainted. To Ronan all that is just a big, bad, boring old cliché. True rock 'n' roll is not about trashing a hotel room or swearing on television - it is about making music for those who follow him, and never failing to deliver the goods.

Sales of over five million records and more female adulation than a mortal man has a right to cannot change this man. As long as the buzz of performing is still there for Ronan, he will remain a music junkie.

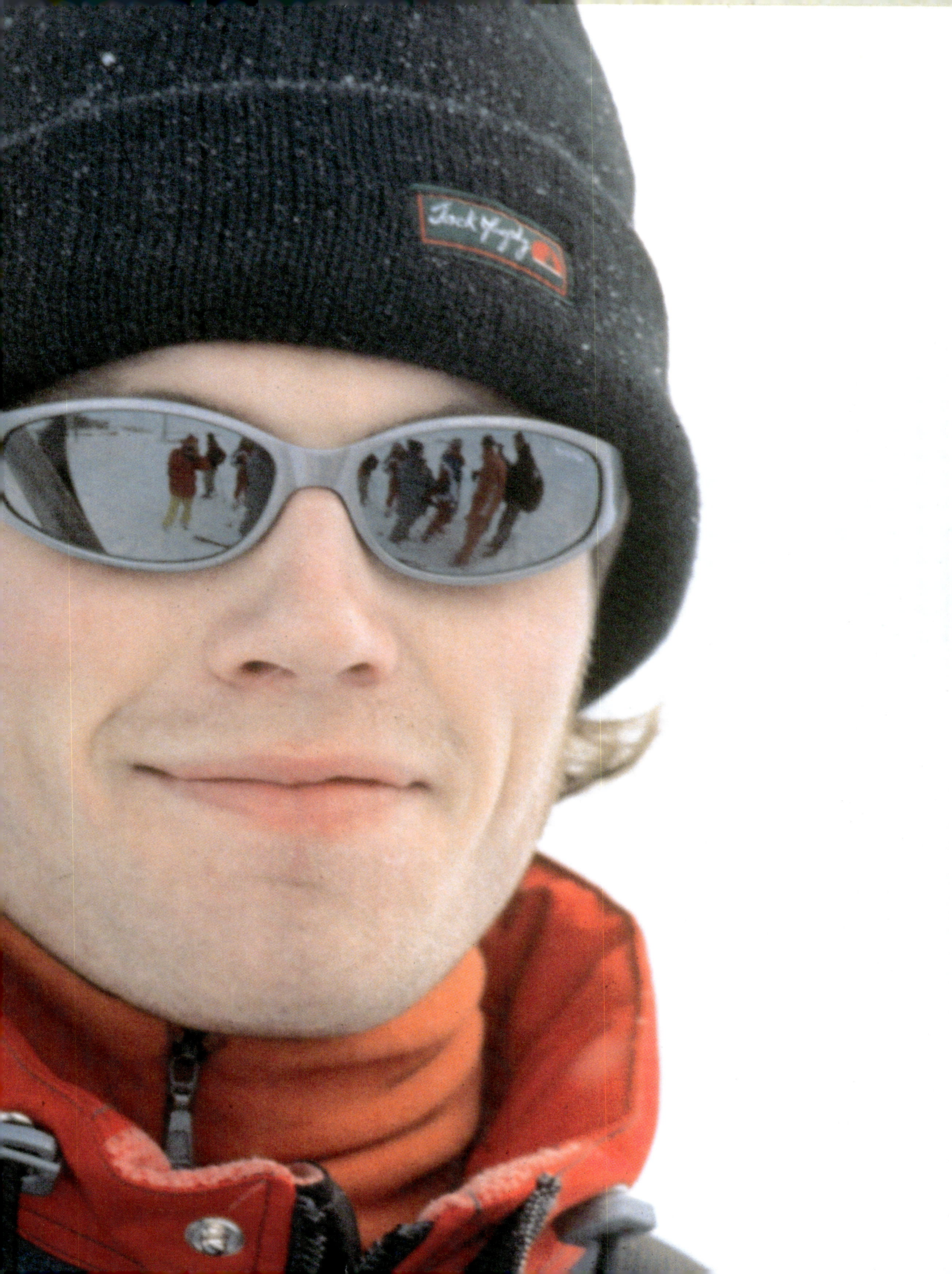

Word has it he is a millionaire, and judging by his record sales, flash cars and enormous mansion, that may well be true. But he has not travelled so far simply for these material possessions. He started life poor but comfortable, and will always remember that the key to a happy life is to have supportive people around you. In his experience of stardom, he has realised that money and fame do not guarantee happiness. He has seen this in many of his peers, most notably in his idol, ex-Take That star Robbie Williams. Underneath that jovial personality and smile, lies a man shrouded by depression, forever battling a drink and drugs problem. Ronan is not going to follow in his footsteps. The day fame and fortune start to take a dangerous toll on his personal state of mind, he will give it all up there and then. As long as he has Yvonne, a little caravan on the beach, his dogs and his memories, he will be able to sleep at night with a smile on his face.

But that seems unlikely for a long while. Within five years he has gone from strength to strength, height to height, old formulas to different beats, and whatever he does, wherever he goes, he has established himself enough to ensure he will always be the best. That is the future. At present, Ronan Keating is just how we like him. Happy, hip, happening and hunky, and as long as those lips smile, those eyes glitter, those toes twinkle and that voice smooches, Ronan will forever stay the most fanciable bloke of our time. Altogether now: one, two, three, phwoooar!

RONAN ON AND ON